The Sequelae of Trauma
A Book of Poems
Liza Ingram

LKG Publishing

Contents

Acknowledgements

This book is a collaborative effort between me and my friend S. Guingona. I wrote the poetry, created the concept and learned how to self publish. She added her flavour to the mix with her editing skills and art creations and long interesting hangouts where I watched her over video chat, while she explored the Washington shore line. Thank you, beauty.

Thank you to my Doctor who made it possible for me to heal by giving me a bridge to humanity, with the primary medicine of common courtesy and human kindness.

For Allen O
and The Sheriff

1

The Sequelae of Trauma

definition...

Sequelae:

From Wikipedia, the free encyclopedia

A **sequelae** is a pathological condition resulting from a disease, injury, therapy or other trauma. A typical sequela is a chronic complication of an acute condition - in other words, a long-term effect of a temporary disease or injury - which follow immediately from the condition. Sequelae can appear long after - even several decades after - the original condition has resolved.

In general, non-medical usage, the terms *sequela* and *sequelae* mean consequence and consequences.

2

Ode to Transference Love

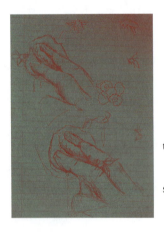

i.
ah... The Doctor...
how I love The Doctor.
let me count the ways:
enchanted by the man cleaning up
the cesspool,
wading into the wounds and as-
sessing the damage
"will she ever work again?"
that is the question...

he sticks his hands in
where the risk of infection is high;
he laughs as things get worse,
the fever rages;
blood and other mysterious fluids
get all over him
but he keeps coming back—
why? why?!
Good Doctor?!
don't you know when to quit?

aren't you fed up with this

'treatment resistant' patient yet?

i wonder, who i am to you?mother? sister? lover?

who are you really trying to save?

you betray yourself,

little tells around the eyes—

i see the animal sometimes...

you drink from the hive

your little touches

so careful

so precise

the palmers' kiss

little bee... he wants the honey

just a taste

just a drop—

a drop is fine!

a drop of medical grade goddess

dribble... dribble... drop... drop... drop...

from finger tip to finger top...

we know the tricks,

you and eye—

we know the tricks of the word and mind

tricks of the flesh — the densest form of the spirit

we know it's the *charge* that matters—

the mechanics mean nothing without the *charge*...

ii.

Doctor! Doctor!

i need your help!

i have too much light

i'm burning from inside

it's bursting out the sides

and going down the wrong lines

there is no one to receive my gift...

(nectar rejected by my previous handler)

now it's rotting inside

like a jersey that hasn't been milked

(udder going septic)

you are akin to a medical leech

draining the post-cervical blood

pooling where infection is an issue

(the cleanup crew

with the unglamorous job

of consuming the degrading tissue)

it tastes like the perfect drug

and is easy to get addicted to

eye see... eye see... oops! you got high off me

as *dirty* as this job might be...

you're helping me!

you're helping me!

3

Darkest Before Dawn

oh, i just want to reject you
frankly, you scare me
i'm quite comfortable in my domain
i just want to protect you
i am unreasonable
but i think that it's all in vain
isn't it supposed to be
darkest before dawn?
how am I supposed to know,
when it's been so long?
what of these night sounds
that have been my lullaby?
my precious tragedy
i don't want to say good bye
but the sun has to rise sometime
'cause isn't it darkest before dawn?
oh, i'm the desperado
but i'm bored with all the lines
i've withdrawn from comfort
one too many times
oh, soothing darkness,

my bitter mistress—

i've grown comfortable

under your rein

but I'm tired of being tired

and I want to love again

the night goes on for a long time,

but not forever

now it's time to say if it's now or never

so wake up and make this dream come true

'cause you get to say when

the hero's gonna be you

the sun has to rise some time

'cause isn't it darkest before dawn?

4

Allen O

i can feel the music coursing
through me
the electric surge of the beat
through my blood
the life force rising rips right
through me
as i connect my hips to the beat—
i think of you
locked into that primal movement
the urge of love moving through us
as we push against the body electric
tsunami inside surging waves
i just want to feel
the throb of your cock inside me
worship me
with your body
you madden me
i want to taste the salt in your
cum
blood

tears
i want to feel that cold bead of sweat
drop
from the knit of your brow
to the pocket under my eye
as you mount and penetrate
the ever opening flower
the blossom in the spring
the japanese aesthetic
unconsummated love
the beginnings and the endings of things
fighting against biology
in this emotional petri dish
restraining the urge
the desire to merge
wings flash
in the mating display
he charms me like a spider
charms his black widow—
any moment
i might bite his head off...

5

Violet Muse

take you where I'm not supposed to
let you underneath my skin
violet muse I'm not opposed to
shoot you up like heroin
disassemble me piece by piece
internally exposed
where I'm not supposed to be
i can't accept this kind of vulnerability
put out the fire
(this is just a fantasy)
thunderheads of the horizon
watch the storm clouds rolling in
the subtle shade of a surface contusion
lightning played like a violin
prick of the needle
guide me like a ventral fin
burning sensation
lightning underneath the skin
cumulating now
dripping from within

violet muse
i shoot you up like heroin
baptismal lace patterns across my eyes
raining down upon me sweet deliverance
from the lies (i tell)
my shadow self run amok
setting fire to my inner shell
medicinal inspiration breaking me out
of this inner hell

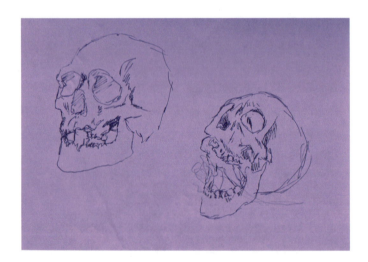

6

White Trash

'i hate to say this,
but you are the superior being...
you can create life'
so he says,
with an amused self-negating grin
it rings beyond respect—
respect would mean equality
this sounds like worship, with the
use of the word

'superior'
why, like this?
behind a wall of clinical glass
when i am used and off limits
like meeting a unicorn
the golden heart
i imagine what you might say to your lover
if you could say such things to a
corn-fed-inbred-redneck-white-trash cockroach
like me...

how is a woman like me,

brutalized by men

my whole life,

starving for basic respect,

how am i supposed to take this?

of course i'm going to fall in love...

why couldn't a man say this to me

when we are between the sheets

why here? it becomes

a harpoon through the heart—

breaking the shell

this bitter elixir to my

butchered soul

it's a map, a light house

a banquet behind bullet proof glass—

now at least i know what food smells like

now at least i know i am starving

as painful as it is

please keep going...

don't stop

Little Bird

for Kelly...

every now and then

there is a bird

that doesn't learn to fly

when its parents push it

from the nest

that is the bird

that will plummet

to its death

(or learn to live on the ground)

8

A Dream for the Doctor

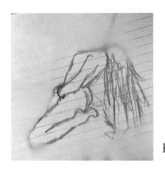

rolling waves of pleasure
the body remembers
vicarious heart lust
the urge for love and approval
bound to the razor-peaks of erotic
pleasure
the merging and explosions of en-
ergy
the mind remembers nothing...
i had a dream about you, Doctor
i dreamt that you grabbed me by the upper arms
and pinned me against the wall
you held your mouth open against my left cheek
and darted your tongue there like a lizard lover
sexy and frightening
you were overpowering me
but I wanted it...

9

Compound Fracture

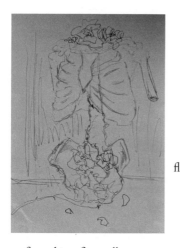

compound fracture
shattered as my stature
i get hard at the sight of softness
rotisserie of saviours
all offering their closure
i want my piece of a pound of
flesh
eyes are just two stars
like healed over scars
death was a voodoo doll

forged in a fire wall
smile jack-o-lantern
paper angels cover the scars
the light was just too far
the light was just too far
poison as an orchid
the daemons thought i tasted good
love's like a rusted violin note
love's like a rusted violin note

...

bloody lace capture
still life of rapture
harlequin figurine of what used to be real
there's traces of flesh underneath the steel
i wish that i was real
i wish that i could feel

so easy to trace
mice know their place

10

Coconuts

washed up on this ocean tide
a shipwrecked soul
living on coconuts and hope
sailor boy
throws me a line
brings me back to shore
brings me back to the world
he wonders why I want to make love to him...

Oedipal Transference to The Doctor

(resulting in dreams and flashbacks)

i feel the line of tension running
from the back of my throat
      down through the knotted insides
of my body and tied right to my clitoris
      the strange pressure that seems to
be cutting me in two
      i see him layered on top of you in an
elaborate flashback—
      the strange dream
      seeing something with one eye
      and something else with another
      a bathtub in one
(with pale walls and blue water)
dark in the other eye
(strange shifting shapes
and this pressure through my vagina
shame pouring inside of me)
cutting me in two
(more than thirty years later...)

i am touching myself

masturbating

34 years old

i can touch myself if i want... right

i look down at my body—

revulsion and shame

i retreat into the mind

your dream hand reaching between my legs

stroking me

damp and electric

a suffocating mask slips over my face

and i am small and you are big

the forbidden spreading over me

in a blanket of heaviness

i am suddenly desperate for your approval

struggling like a little fish against the riptide

to feel this pleasure

to feel this orgasm

the shape of your fingers

reminds me of my daddy's hands

tell me I'm good

say it's okay

i feel the mantle of shame

mixing with orgasm

mixing with dark and light

your face and his overlap—

a soothing balm

to the scorched earth

the acidic shame

that has put a damper

on my whole person

tarred my wings

and hangs on me like an invisible anvil

dragging me down into the depths of the marked whore

what do I do with this,

Doctor?

any ideas?

12

The Container

romance in a petri dish
a culture of the chemistry
between two humans
swabbed and incubated
to produce some kind of
bizarre-mad-lab-scientist
franken-creature feelings...

that can result in laboratory explosions
and cultures taking on
a life of their own...

13

Therapy:

(the eroticized transference)

i want to fuck him so bad
i want his cock in me balls deep
his voice reminds me of my dad's
pussy gushing, as I weep...
i want to be bathed in his bodily fluids
fuck me and be my daddy...
my body becomes sexually aroused around him
now, how's that for therapy?
it's not my fault...
it's not my fault...
please...
please...

i didn't mean to

i'm so sorry for being so very rude

my vagina throbs

my heart races

i struggle with my little-girl needs for a hero

and my woman's desire for him to bend me over his desk

whip out his cock

and take me from behind

i want to tell him all the ways i want to fuck him

and just watch the excitement grow

(he wants to fuck me, i know)

i trigger his 'man instincts'

his body wants to impregnate mine

the animal inflamed

by the close proximity

as i share my deepest

sexual secrets with him

all the eros-energy flying around

creates a fierce and diving force

a spiritual alchemy

swirling in the tension

of apposing urges

change affects

transformation ensues

the butterfly is triggered

to emerge from the cocoon

the electric sexual feeling I get

reminds me of the way my dad

used to purr into the back of my neck

14

Forest for the Trees

love seemed such a fallacy
an unforgiving fantasy
until you came and spoke to me
your words were such a sooth-
ing dream
who knew, who knew?

not i! it's true
who knew i wouldn't be on my own?
who knew your love would make this my home?
'cause i can't see the forest for the trees
it's just the way you say that you love me
oh, how you put my heart at ease
it's just the way you say that you love me
that i should find such sanctuary
sleeping in the cemetery
writing my obituary
spring forth something so contrary
and cracked my heart
(its morbid shell)
and woke me from my nightmare spell

with a kiss that did dispel
and found a spring to drill a well
the petals of my heart unfold
your light, the sun, my eyes behold
to see what in my garden grows
your love that plants the seeds I sow

15

Forget-Me-Not

every time daddy hit us
we broke off a piece
to forget
because we loved daddy
forgive and forget
now the broken parts
live in the oubliette

16

Art Porn

i want to fuck his brains out
i want to slip under the table
and unzip his pants
and suck his cock
until he shoots it in my mouth
hot and soapy
washing my mouth out
because i've been such a bad girl
i want you to bend me over your
desk
slip it in me hard and hot
you have a dick i am not afraid
of
such a rare bird
it's always the soul that i want
you can taste the soul through the cock

17

Electra

nowhere can i go
to relieve this ache
no release
no relief
except for the constant desire
to handle myself
i keep it together
the animal i tether—

checkmate the instinctual urge
to merge
with your flesh
my under-thoughts whisper
what your paternal threshold
would be—
father
i figured
a kaleidoscope
underneath your skin
i want to see
the restrains

madden me

i know what the boys want

i'm confused when they don't try to fuck me

...

thank God you're a country boy...

18

Pygmalion

i show up the suit your wear
prune the branches whose fruit you cannot bare
i am your bonsai tree
fall in love with me
playing God with my heart
your disapproval is razor sharp
your notion of what is right,
is it worth the fight?
you can take the girl out of the country,
but you can't take the country out of the girl
pygmalion,
pygmalion—
i can't sleep in your world
your servant cast
serf class
my face is my fortune
my father was an orphan
we know mice know their place
which mask would you like to be my face
shaping me to walk amongst your kind
don't fall in love with your sculpture

the brittle mask won't stand the test of time
see beneath the mask
see the soul inside...

...

a diamond dropped in the mud is still a diamond....

19

Bad Girl

i want the devil to come
and love me with his drug love—
his morphine hands
and opium kisses
fill me with what is forbidden
ah... like the bad girl i am,
fill me with your drug love
make this darkness go away
come have your dolly to play with...
i want his valium voice
words stroke me like velvet
with his fork tongue he gives me
forty lashes
laps up my sins like milk
scraping on the ground
scraping on the ground
devil! give it to me now
i can feel you, somehow

Id

so do i let the thoughts out unedited—

or do i refine them first before they hit the page,

a kind of prerecorded compression?

a brave move, perhaps?

i am often afraid

to let the more

feeble voices speak,

the kind that squawk obscenities

like a caged parrot,

neurotic and balding in spots

from the nervous habit of

plucking its feathers out

the strange primordial desires
emerge from my subconscious
i want to touch
The Doctor's penis
i want to give him
a blow job
bend the knee
the words push their way
to the surface
and hover there...
... building momentum
and the accompanying images
and sensations
it flares up in me
like a psychic erection
i will see the image
through the lens of
my mind's eye
kneeling in front of him
unzipping his pants
taking the head of his cock
in my mouth
like i was sipping wine
straight from the bottle
(i think that is what is happening
when one is sucking cock)
there is the drinking of magic
straight from the source
of the life force
taking great pulls of some

tangible pleasure

i always love it

in my mouth—

getting so close to it

the great man spread

coupling him inside me

in my mouth

plugged right into

the pulse of pleasure

that would pour through him

just a few buttons

zippers

cloth

a few feet of space

a desk

and some social rules

separate us

from performing

this relic ritual

that was formed and functional

before rational thought

was a twinkle of creation

in the evolutionary eye

he has seduced the animal in me

the loyal bitch in heat

the body not cooperating with reason

i feel the throb in my pussy for him

my mind cannot reconcile the urge

... and our place,

and our speech,

i just want The Doctor
to bend me over
push up my skirt
pull down my panties
spit on his hand
and slip is fingers in
to see how wet I am
he undoes his pants
strokes his cock in hand
before he pushes in
and we are locked together—
bonded as one
in the flesh

... why?
why am I like this?

21

Siren

he sees the goddess in me
i was sleeping
when i look through his eyes
he gave me self esteem
he is lifting me out of slavery
my mind
my heart

were in a cage
and he picked the locks
and set us free
and the paradox is:
i am more fragile
and more vulnerable now
i need him more than ever
he is protecting me from getting
picked up by another handler
he is liberating
the goddess in chains
the sirens of the sea
calling the sailors to the rocks
maybe they were calling for help...

The Sequelae of a Lifetime of Whoredom

oh, such a golden heart
i want to taste it
grip it in my harpy talons
and draw the blood of the virgin
drink of the communion innocence
to cure my raging soul infection
Doctor, give me this injection
i can see the shadows
flickering around your eyes
i can smell the hormones
and feel the heat rise...

want to play Doctor?

you like the catholic girls...

maybe a little pleated skirt

we could play pretend

just a little flirt

you could discipline me

c'mon, who could we possibly hurt?

a whore's heart is a hinged fossilized thing

that just swings open

to let pass the stream of suffering

i need you to use me

fuck and abuse me

stick it right through me

otherwise what's the use of me?

what are you doing?

... what I'm good at...

give a whore respect

(mind you, an alien concept...)

she might want to reward you with a little party

(on the house)

...

how could you possibly be friends with a hooker?

you have a wife...

Afterword

I started therapy in 2017 after a many trips to the hospital for mysterious chest pains. The hospital doctors could not find anything mechanically wrong with my heart but sent me to the local cardiology clinic for more testing. I was assigned a doctor who had the same finding but he said that the issue was a psychiatric one. Knowing how little help was available to complicated, high functioning, low income patients like me, he offered to take me on as a patient and see if he could help me in some way.

We started simply by documenting some of the major trauma that had occurred and assessing the damage. I had been trafficked in a martial arts cult, as a teenager, so we started with that. Through the process of telling him what happened to me I started to receive the therapeutic benefit of talk therapy even though he was not experienced with that kind of treatment. I had never felt safe with a man before. Especially a man like him. He was older and in a position of authority. I thought that men like him were on a different team.

My doctor and I set in motion the beginnings of a great healing journey together that results from the doctor witnessing and supporting my pain and forming a relationship with me, the patient, and out of sheer necessity, using the relationship as the medicine. My doctor built with me the first trusting relationship I had ever experienced with a man and that was the clutch treatment that ultimately brought an end to my anxiety attacks and a host of other symptoms that I suffered from.

I developed an intense sexual attraction and a deep love for him. This is called an erotic transference and it was so visceral and intense it would cause sometimes my body to shake during treatment and would eventually reveal the presence of alter personalities that were containing trauma far worse than I had known. In January of 2018 I was diagnosed with dissociative identity disorder. It was a very stigmatizing and disturbing label but served its purpose to create a pathway for treatment and healing. As a way of dealing with my feelings I wrote poetry about my experiences and that is how this work came about. The process of me sharing my feelings and poetry with him created even more healing circumstances. I was very fortunate to have someone handle the situation with such patience and empathy and support the environment I needed to make lasting changes to my nervous system and psyche.

Erotic transference is a well known phenomenon in psychology that has been documented all the way back to the very early days of Sigmund Freud and Josef Breuer and forms as a result of the patient forming an attachment to the clinician. If managed correctly then the erotic transference is a powerful tool for transformation and healing albeit a very challenging one. My doctor was a very honourable person and I was very safe expressing all my feelings to him. I learned from Kirk Honda, a notable expert clinician from Seattle, who has an amazing podcast called "Psychology in Seattle", that the attachment process that we go through as children is critical to the development of the self and a healthy mental environment and that the patterns in the relationships we form as children are destined to be repeated in our adult relationships. Because the relationship that I had with my parents did not meet my emotional needs, I ended up being vulnerable to predators and people with abusive and controlling tendencies. I did not know what a healthy relationship looked like so I could not identify when I was being treated poorly. Through the process of developing a relationship in this therapeutic environment I was able to achieve tremendous growth and finally rid myself of all controlling and abusive relationships. Even though these poems are a bit vulgar and express a lot of pain and grief they are ultimately a testament to healing.

About the author

Liza Ingram is a writer, burlesque dancer, musician and a mother to one son. She makes a living as a tailor by day. She lives in Peterborough, Ontario. Follow her on Instagram @shadow.dancer888

Shadow Dancer is her stage name and the name of one of her alters.

She has written about her experiences suffering from Dissociative Identity Disorder and human trafficking in her up coming book, Hydra. It is set to be published in 2025.

BONUS MATERIAL: An excerpt chapter from Hydra is included at the end of this publication.

23

Hydra: A Memoir (BONUS! Chapter Preview)

Hydra:

Definition from the Merriam-Webster dictionary:

1. a many-headed serpent or monster in Greek mythology that was slain by Hercules and each head of which when cut off was replaced by two others

1. a multifarious evil not to be overcome by a single effort

1. a southern constellation of great length that lies south of Cancer, Sextans, Corvus, and Virgo; and is represented on old maps by a serpent

1. any of numerous small tubular freshwater hydrozoan polyps (*Hydra* and related genera) having at one end a mouth surrounded by tentacles; via Latin from Greek *hudra,* "water snake"; named by Linnaeus because, if cut into pieces, each section can grow into a whole animal

An electric fence is just a psychological barrier for a cow. The wires run along the wooden posts holding a voltage charge. Ours was 16,000 volts. It was supposed to be enough juice to stop a bear. A cow is a vast behemoth of a creature, thousands of pounds of muscle and bone perched on powerful cutting hoofs. A small cow could trample an electric fence with little effort if it was willing to suffer a shock. But the cow falls to the path of least resistance and avoids pain as much as possible. This is how humans keep cows contained so easily.

I watched a tiny goat walk straight through an electric fence because he had the understanding that if he just took a bit of pain there was freedom waiting on the other side. A goat made a cost vs. risk assessment right in front of me and came out the winner. That's how smart they are. We called this particular goat Billy Houdini, because every night we would pen him in somewhere—in the barn, inside of a mesh of wires, behind locked doors—and every morning he would be standing in the courtyard waiting for us to come and play with him. Somehow, as if by magic, he'd escape.

January 17, 2021

It's red wine tonight. That's not even my style. I usually drink white. I don't like to stain my teeth. I'm too vain and it doesn't look good on camera. I gotta keep the dream alive. It's peak COVID outside and we are in the midst of the second lockdown. I am trying to outrun my depression with art, driving myself back to the keyboard to make another attempt at writing this godforsaken book. What do I have to lose? My power to be right, I guess. If I don't try, then I can't fail. Or, truly, I can't succeed. The belief that I am defective and bad fits me like a Skyn condom fits a man about to give you the business. I had to drink just to get here because I know that this time might be the time. The moment when I dissect myself for the sake of exposition. Expose my defects for the sake of art, science and a chance to do something that matters—maybe just to me. But it's my dream at stake here. It's my life on the examining table. The sense of meaning and purpose that comes from writing something is just too fulfilling for me to approach sensibly. I have to get a bit buzzed first. I know that there is something brewing in the abyss. Something crawling in the dark matter of my private universe that is controlling this outcome.

I just spent the last four hours jerking my literary clit to Henry Miller's pivotal book, The Tropic of Cancer. It was as good as I had expected, a book that is mostly a feverish dream caught on paper. I let the subtle savagery of Miller's writing work me like a prostitute of the English language. There was a sinister familiarity in the words that wrapped around my brain and infected it with imagery like an aggressive STI. I am still trying to shake off some of it. It was too good. Too vivid. It might give me nightmares.

It is my goal to write the shittiest book. The worst book in the world. I will try my hardest to write the shittiest book I can. Then

I would be doing a whole lot more than what I have been doing for the last 25 years—just starts and stops. Nothing is finished. I just keep practising. I keep rehearsing for the main event.

I like to think I am good. Here inside my bubble, I am protected from the outside world, growing like an embryo into a fetus. But I hold back the birth. There is not a limit on gestation in the literary world. Book babies can grow on and on and then die in the womb. I can still feel the kick. It pushes against my insides and reminds me that it's not dead, that no amount of hardship can kill it. It just feeds on danger and drama. Swollen and monstrous now, it signals that it's going to be born. My ugly book baby. I will love it as much as a real baby. So if it's born alive, I will put it out to the world, no matter how deformed and grotesque it is.

It's all Miller's fault. He got me hooked on a good metaphor again. I had fallen down the bottomless pit of technology and I forgot my roots. The writing. The naked sentence. I am jealous of this man and his art. He seemed like a grotesque figure. A womanizer. A sleaze bag through and through. I probably would have loved him. That seems to be the case for me. I find one good quality in a man and that's all I really need. It's a tragic character flaw. My heart is much, much sluttier than my pussy. All my heart requires is a drop of kindness to fall in love. It's not fair.

My heart is a razor ball that hangs in my chest. The slightest inter-action with a man will cut me. He just has to breathe in my direction and I will suffer. Yet still, I want a man to love me. I hold out and hope that someday I will feel what it's like to be loved. There is hope for me yet.

It's all The Doctor's fault. He lit the pilot light of hope in my heart. This story might be about that relationship. It's the only way I will ever be able to trap him: in between the pages of a book. I will immortalize him like Shakespeare immortalized his male lover in a sonnet.

He has given me a substance that resembles love in the form of his attention. I can't tell if it's real or synthetic, but it has a similar effect. And let's be honest here, how would I ever be able to tell the difference? He just kept feeding me like a stray cat, his ridiculous belief that he could help me if he just kept trying. It was all his fault. I trusted him. He should have never been so reliable. He was the one who told me that I could come back to his office as long as I thought he was helping me. What a dumb thing to say.

To his credit, he didn't know at the time. He thought I was normal. Maybe even gifted. He thought I was going to be an easy patient. He said that to me as I was about to leave our first session. "Oh, you're going to be easy." I didn't have the heart to tell him. I wanted to believe him. I wanted it to be easy for him.

But I knew.

I knew that many had tried and all had failed to help me.

***

It's peak COVID out, and as I write, it's technically illegal to go out for unofficial reasons. It's hard to know what is really going on with any kind of certainty. With the amount of corruption I have seen in my life, conspiracy seems plausible, but I can't know or draw a hard conclusion about anything. There is hardly anything to hold onto right now. We are told to stay home. I will do as I am told for the most part, until it becomes too much. Apparently cases are rising and people are dying. I live alone and sometimes don't see people for days. It's not so hard to follow protocol when one is naturally isolated. All the things I liked to do are banned now, but I seem to eat adversity for breakfast. I was bred on limitations and making do. Why should that be any different now?

When I wear a mask, I think of it as altitude training. Until I start to suffocate. Thank God I don't work in the service industry.

January 19, 2021

I am so tired now. It's not even that late and I feel like I could just drift into a stupor. I could just lie in bed and let myself be soothed by Netflix reruns of my favourite '90s dramas. I am just going through the motions right now. My brain is too fried to form a real literary project. I have to do endless scales instead. It's part of my problem. I have a medical condition that makes my brain like a living Etch A Sketch. I walk away and I come back a different person. It's so disappointing in some ways. It wreaks havoc on my ability to finish a project.

I will not accept defeat. I will keep pushing to make something of myself. I know I have all the pieces, it's just getting enough perspective to get them all together. It's my heart that stops me. My butchered heart. I am amazed at the way it beats in my chest. Despite being pummelled by the world, it goes on. But it hurts.

I keep trying. I sit in front of the keyboard again. I pound out the keys. I try to make the words pour smoothly from my mind onto the screen and do everything I can to keep training this muscle. I'm like Rocky. I don't care what the rounds look like as long as I go the distance. I know I will be able to make something out of this skill someday. I wonder if I am going to be able to do it. I keep getting interrupted. I will write something today, and then when I go back to it, the slate is clean. It's a new day and I am a blank slate. I try to have faith that it will happen. My intention will be enough to bring it back. There are too many voices talking to me at once. They all want to be a part of it, now.

How do we untangle this mess? How do we try to conquer this mountain? I know that despondency and defeat will not make the dream come true. I have talent and I want it to amount to something. So right now, I write shit. I will just keep silently screaming into a blank page until something eventually comes of it. I will try to shape this word, this intention, but it's so hard. I press on into the blizzard of sadness that threatens to engulf me and I try to fight it by describing what it feels like.

It's a blurry madness—TV static snow that sneaks up on me and baits me to give up the fight, to give into Netflix and inertia and the comfort of being right, even if it's pathetic, even when I haven't tried my best. I parry the sword of defeat by another sentence. I push through this massive weight I carry around my neck, telling myself: *I am a viking. I am a warrior.* All the thoughts of sadness and defeat sit just outside the small shelter I have made, and I try to put thought to word, like striking a fragile flint on a small stretch of cold steel, hoping to catch a spark. Try to spin straw into gold.

***

And I feel myself floating away. A balloon for a head. My head expands until my eyes lose focus and I don't know what I am saying anymore. I have become a master of forgetting.

I saw the snow today. The snow that fell down through the air. The snow that swirls through the air like tiny feathered dancers. The sound becomes dry and you can't hear any sound reflections. An isolation booth of snow. I feel my Dad's spirit haunting me through the snow. I am transported back in time. Back onto the farm of my youth.

When I was eleven, we moved out to the country, to a farm that was near a town that was so small they had a veterinary clinic but not a real store you could shop at. There wasn't even a place to get coffee. Just a school and a vet. Everything else you had to make the trip into town for. It was here that my dad captured me in the snow globe.

The snow was circling around us, a frosty silent audience. We walked at twilight dusk. The sky was a mysterious shade of pink that seemed to radiate from the clouds. He tackled me, taking me to the ground. I fought back and we rolled around, breaking up the banks. In the pause between childhood and adolescence, I could still play with him in such a manner without any strangeness. My body was still flat and non-threatening. We stretched out hand to hand and swished snow angels with our limbs. He pulled me into an embrace and together we stared into the sky.

"I will frame this moment and keep it forever," he whispered into my ear, and the hair on the back of my neck stood up. A radiant love engulfed me. And I wished we could stay in that bliss forever. "I love you."

"I love you, too."

I think I have often dreamt of this place, so full of magic and terrors.

January 20, 2021

I woke up early this morning. It's five-oh-one. I woke up suffering from worry. The dream rats of disaster were gnawing at my brain, making little bleeds in my ability to sleep. I tried to curl into the bed, to feel the cheap mattress hold me up against the world. It was to no avail. I grew desperate and I prayed to the endless inner space. The murky depth of mystery. I imagined angels surrounding me filling me with light. I prayed to Jesus. How do I know that an answer from Jesus is an actual answer and not a product of my own mental illness? There is no way of separating the demons from the angels except by their actions.

I hear voices. I react to imaginary tigers like they are laying their long teeth, cold and bitter, on the back of my neck.

My body will keep trying to run away—
Kick.
Scream.
Fight.
Frozen still.
—while my conscious mind will be painfully aware that there is no tiger. The tiger is just a teddy bear. Or my son trying to get my attention.

It hurts to live.

I figure it won't hurt to pray to Jesus.

If the delusions of my mind come up with a solution to my suffering, then maybe they are useful.

There were words in my head, streams of them, before I could get to the keyboard.

Someone in here was reminding me not to get any ideas about my greatness. I like to think that I am a great artist, suffering for my art. It is not something I have chosen. I did not go into the life of pain so that I would emerge something great. I was just dumped here. I was abandoned here.

I have met the devil.

I know his name.

ED. The Farmer. A demon. Like something out of Twin Peaks, but with a pitch fork.

He kept me as his pet.

I used to think that it was only The Farmer that caused me to bleed internally, but I know now that the suffering started much earlier. It started in the womb with conception. My parents were great sufferers. But back then, misery was the norm and no one had any idea that there would be anything different. It was my parents' hope for a better life for me that may have caused the most acute agony. They gave me this idea that my life was going to be so much better than theirs. I will likely black out before I can dump the bulk of my pain on this page.

Unglamorous typing. Not sweet and romantic like graceful long-hand, the sweet old fashioned ballet of writing. I worry about the children not learning long-hand. How will they hide their journals from the world now? Now, they just post it on Facebook and let their bloody wounds infect the masses. Back in my day, we hid our pain in a thorough cake of denial. My elders would never let me complain so hard, no matter how much I was bleeding.

My parents made the mistake of telling me I was special. Early on, before shit hit the fan, they gave me the impression that I had some kind of dazzling power and that I would go on to do great things. This idea warmed me through the darkest of nights. But now this dream is just a silver cobweb collecting dust and I am sympathetic to the spiders that are making their home there. It's a persistent dream. A psychiatric soother.

It seems like a proper delusion that I can no longer cling to. I can no longer hold onto the idea that "someday I am going to do something great." That someday has arrived. That happens in one's thirties: the great threat of death opens its eyes. I realize now that it was here the whole time, but I couldn't see it through the shiny optimism of youth.

It's my hormones that are doing this. I am bitter because I wanted more babies to be distracted by.

My dreams to be married with a big happy family were burnt to the ground. The story is too long for me to start. I am afraid I will black out. The curse of my condition. The mind is shaken and brought back to a flat grey modelling surface.

I was reminded by some bitter voice this morning not to confuse anything I do with art. I am just a neanderthal drawing pictures in the mud pretending I am painting the Mona Lisa. The voice was very clear not to get aggrandize about just how clever and talented I am, just to keep making silly pictures.

Enjoy picture making. Just play with the mud. Don't be an artist.

I am much too poor to be a real artist.

My butchered brain has allowed me to receive my tiny government trust fund. I fit the bar for "damaged enough" to not have to work again for a long time. In order to make a living at writing, I would have to have some kind of talent. I am seeing some ability to string something of a sentence together, but how can that talent co-oscillate into a true waveform enough for anyone to hear it when I am constantly getting cut off?

To be truthful, I don't even know who is writing this. I don't even know my own name right now. I think it's Shadow.

I should tell you, I have multiple personalities.

A real live Sybil.

It's a reverse Fight Club. There is no suspense building. You don't need to figure it out. It's just out there—like a premature baby.

I left the keyboard to get a coffee and now the Etch A Sketch is blank again. Where was I? What was I saying? Who is this? What planet am I on? Simple words. Simple sentences. The work of the neanderthal.

I woke up this morning at 4am. Suffering. It's COVID out. The lockdown is imminent and oppressive. So mournful is the population that no one is even complaining about it on Facebook.

It's a layer of oppression that I don't need. I have had enough servitude and slavery to last a lifetime. I just got out of my prison. I was out only one year and the world just collapsed. And not a fun Mad Max kind of collapse, but a smokey evaporation of the normal freedoms. Now, going for a walk with a friend is breaking the law. At least in war times, you could visit your friends. You could huddle with your family in an attic. Now, you have to stay six feet apart and wear masks.

This tragic polarization of the populace is causing an already sick society to get even sicker. If you ever read even a hair of Freud, you will come to realize that the ills of society are something that humans have been complaining about for a while.

So many voices all of a sudden.
I can be naked here.
No one has to see.
I hear them.
It hurts.
My brain is an Etch A Sketch. It's getting wiped now.

Fear is a great lathering agent. I am scared I will love this book baby too much and I will publish it, and then the world will know just how mediocre I am. But I have to remember that I am just a speck of dust. No one is going to read this. I am not any great literary talent. I am just a neanderthal playing in the mud. Drawing crude pictures of the scary dreams I have had. I am small and non-threatening.

Let's talk about The Blacksmith.

Because he is just a daydream. He is just a fantasy. A beautiful man that is not interested in me. We had the tragic fate of meeting on Tinder. I was swiping to pass the time. Trying to move on from some other Tinder date who had just broken my thin glass heart by canceling last minute. It's truly a handicap to be this sensitive and yet still have hope for love.

Silly, silly girl.
I still blame The Doctor.
Stupid Doctor.
I guess we will talk about The Blacksmith later.

July 2001

My mother kept her promise to drive us into town every day for school if we moved into the farmhouse with her. It was a twenty-minute drive from the small farming community where we lived to the nearest city where I went to school.

The stereo system in her car had the best speakers our family ever owned, so we took advantage of the transit to blast our favourite music. Over the last year, through the process of constant exposure, my siblings and I had conditioned our mother to enjoy the dissonant music of Nine Inch Nails and Marilyn Manson. She was already a fan of Black Sabbath and Iron Maiden and other old metal bands, so it wasn't a huge jump. Anyone traveling the country back roads that happened to pass us would be assaulted by the raging of Pretty Hate Machine and Antichrist Superstar much earlier in the morning than was tasteful.

I liked living on the farm because the house was large and a relic of the 1950s. When we first moved in, the family before us had let the house go completely, and we had to spend hours scrubbing all the surfaces with a pungent citrus soap that stained the tips of my fingers a pale orange. The parcel of land that we lived on was located in the middle of a small suburb in a tiny town in the middle of rural Ontario.

Being cut off from my newly formed social circle was the only draw-back that I found from living there. I was in the twelfth grade, and for the first time in my high school career I had found a group of friends that I could relate to. Even though I didn't pierce my body or artistically scar my skin or wear goth makeup the way they did, I liked the way they didn't seem to care what other people thought about them.

For the past three years, I had maintained a grade point average of 4.0 or better. The blossoming of my social life, however, had come with a price. Smoking dope and having fun with my new friends became much more interesting than getting to class on time. The danger of being able to write my own notes had become apparent with the amount of time I had been truant. However, my previous reputation and rapport with the teachers saved me from getting into any serious trouble. I was skilled at making friends with my teachers, and I found that many of them really didn't want to bust me despite being witness to my academic demise.

I remember walking into my OAC (grade thirteen) music class so high that the wall paper looked like it was rippling in a psychedelic tide. There was no way that my teacher didn't notice I was ripped. He was a child of the '70s and would've probably seen high people before. He might have even been high himself. He was kind enough not to embarrass me, but in retrospect, it might have been nice to have someone draw attention to the way I was suddenly not caring about my future. At the time, however, I would have died of embarrassment. I had no interest in changing my ways if I got caught but I would simply resolve to be more stealth about it.

The summer following twelfth grade was loaded with the challenge of getting into town every day. My dad lived in the city, so I always had a place to stay if I needed it. I had other places I could go, but my dad's was a sure thing. I didn't always like going there because he was a terrible housekeeper and there was always the claustrophobic smell of stale urine and rotting food floating around the house. He was too cheap to hire a housekeeper but insisted on grilling me to do the cleaning whenever I stayed over there.

***

I had a friend who was more sexually experienced than me, and on this particular night, we were downtown trying to get laid. I wasn't sure if we were serious or not, but it was a fun game to play. We had left her parents' house declaring our intentions. I was so horny it was painful. No amount of masturbation seemed to relieve this constant sexual tension that permeated my body and actually caused me pain

"I'm so horny, dude. I gotta get laid tonight," my friend said.

"I know man. I don't know what I'll do if I don't get some action."

"We're gonna do it tonight. You gotta mean it this time. You're the oldest virgin I know."

"Shut up!!" I was the only virgin I knew except for my little sister who was twelve. It seemed to hang on me like an albatross.

In my circle of friends, nobody was a virgin. BDSM was the cool thing to do. We would often get together in small groups and play PG-ish versions of "Slave and Master." We even had slave names and wrote each other devotional love letters in "slavespeak." Through it all, I never had intercourse. I was all for doing it. It seemed like I had been born horny and puberty had turned me into an oozing pile of hormones. My incredible social awkwardness had thwarted any chance I had of hooking up with anyone and put me in a rather miserable predicament.

That year, I had come to the conclusion that I was bisexual. Though my sexual attraction to women was rampant, unfortunately I was even more awkward with women than I was with men. We lived in a small town and still it wasn't socially acceptable to be openly gay or bi—except within the tiny clique I had fallen into by the power of my younger brother, who was a social ninja. He had been my backstage pass to cool. He was constantly coaching me and I was making a little progress. At least I didn't hide in the bathroom at lunch time anymore, eating with my legs tucked up on the toilet seat.

It was dark when we had left her house but it wasn't a far walk to downtown. Where we lived there wasn't much to do if you were under age except drink, do drugs, destroy things or have sex.

The street lights traced pale yellow patterns on the roads and we walked on the dark side of the street so people couldn't see us. Of course, we were dressed in all black. You could walk anywhere in town in twenty minutes if you kept up a good pace, and it didn't take us long to get to the downtown strip. We were headed to the fountain where, for some reason, there always seemed to be a crowd of drunken youth looking to blow off steam.

When we arrived, there was a cluster of teen-ish boys stumbling around, smashing bottles on the sidewalk. They were talking but I didn't really follow the conversation. My friend seemed to know them and they hooted and high-fived her enthusiastically.

"Hey, ladies!" one of the less inebriated of the group said. He was blond and tall with a narrow beakish face. He wasn't exactly handsome but his eyes were kind. He seemed to be a light hearted low income ex-skater, and I saw him as somewhat simple. I decided that if he made a move I would probably sleep with him. "What are you up to tonight?" he said to us.

"Hi, N—" she said. His short friend sidled up beside him. "Who's your friend?" my friend asked, took a pack of Players Light King Size out of her purse and tapped out a smoke. "You want one?" she said, looking my way. I took a smoke from her and held it awkwardly between my fingers.

"Oh, this is B—" said the tall one, and his short friend smiled at us and nodded slightly. "Hey, one of you guys got a light?" she asked, and Tall fumbled in his pockets to retrieve a Zippo. He rolled it on his jeans and lit both of our cigarettes.

"Hey, we're looking to get laid tonight," my friend said to them.

"Oh, are you, now?" Tall smiled crookedly. "Well, John's lookin' to hook up." He pointed to a young man who was calmly standing on the side of the fountain holding his penis and pissing into the circular well

of shining water. I could see his face in the dim moonlight. Some God had blessed him with chiseled even features. He looked like he could be a double lead with Leo DiCaprio. We all stood speechless as he finished up his stream and raised his hands over his head, double punching the air. He shouted and jumped off the side of the fountain, positioned himself as if to take a drink and plunged his head into the fouled water. The drunken crowd cheered. Tall and Short started laughing.

"No," my friend said. "You want him, Liza?"

"No, I'm okay." I just couldn't do it. Not after the head-dunking-piss-fountain display.

"Awe, he's just havin' a good time, girls. He's on leave from the army right now."

That didn't change anything for me. My friend changed the subject.

"So, what are you guys up to tonight?" she said.

"Oh, we're just out trying to have a good time, too. You guys wanna burn one?"

"Does a bear shit in the woods?" she said. The group of drunken young men circled around their urine baptized ringleader in a way that reminded me of a scene from Lord of the Flies.

"Well, let's get out of here, then. C'mon, we'll go over to the park." He gestured to us to follow. We crossed the street and walked towards the park.

We didn't succeed in getting laid that night. Both of us were too timid to seduce the polite young men that got us high. I was surprised that my friend, with all her experience, hadn't been more aggressive. But maybe she just didn't want it that bad.

The walk home from the park was fun, with the edge of reality blurred from the marijuana. We had worked up a solid appetite by the time we found our way to my dad's front door. We had agreed to stay overnight at my house because my friend's curfew was 11:00 and we headed home around 12:30.

I refused to have a curfew and came and went as I pleased. My father tried to enforce a curfew on me once and I extricated myself from his house and moved in with my mother. My parents both had a tendency to enforce rules at their own emotional whim, rather than have clear solid boundaries. My siblings and I tended to keep to rules that would keep our parents' feelings from getting hurt and allow us to continue to do as we pleased. For example, we would lie about our drug use to our father but we would share our stash with our mother so that both parents would be happier.

I was greeted in the kitchen by the typical mess of dirty dishes and leftovers of dinner rotting on the stove. My friend took a seat at the kitchen table and I started to rummage through the cupboards to find something decent to eat. I didn't know if my dad was home, but part of me wished that he wasn't, because the house tended to be much calmer and more predictable when he was at work.

"Dude, I am so hungry." my friend said.

"Yeah, me too. I don't know what we got here." I opened the fridge and was greeted by the smell of mold and milk gone bad. I quickly closed it and tried the freezer. I found some cheap frozen TV dinners that would hit the spot. I decided not to have one because I had recently gone on a diet that didn't include wheat. These cheap freezer meals didn't look like diet food to me. I opted for an orange that was hiding amongst the rubble on the counter.

I had pulled a dinner from the freezer and had situated it on the counter when my father's face suddenly loomed from the darkness beyond the kitchen doorway. I could tell right away that he was in a bad mood.

"What are you doing eating my food?" His voice sounded bearish and slurred as if he had been drinking, but my father never drank. The slight slurring came from his Newfie accent that only resurfaced when he was in a rage.

"My friend and I were hungry!" I said. I was unable to control my anger. "It's a 99¢ TV dinner, Dad! C'mon!"

He opened the fridge door and slammed it, storming out of the kitchen and back into the cave-like dark of the living room, a golem creature, the only light coming from the flickering of the TV. I grabbed a knife to open the dinner and stopped, hovering over the sink. I pressed the knife into my arm. I was so angry I wanted to cut myself.

His constant switching of moods had been particularly bad this week. One day I would be his princess and could do no wrong, and the next I was a vile leech that was sucking up his resources trying to make him go broke. Tonight, for some reason, I was out of patience. I threw down the dinner and the knife and followed him into the living room where he had retreated back into his easy chair and started to surf the channels.

"What's your problem? You're embarrassing me in front of my friend." I normally retreated in the face of his rage but couldn't this time. Tears welled up in my eyes as I looked at him.

"I don't want her in my house. She's not a good friend. She's a waste of skin," he hissed. His face was contorted with anger and hatred and he clenched his fists as he spoke. I looked up and, to my horror, my friend had followed me into the war zone and was standing a few feet behind the chair.

"Dad, she can hear you!"

"No, she can't!" he shouted back at me. He was angry at her because of a fight she and I had had several months ago. I'd made the mistake of talking about it and he had carried a grudge against her ever since. I couldn't quite decide if he was doing this out of spite or if he was so blind

from his mood that he honestly didn't think she could hear him. I could see her standing a few feet behind his chair. The dining room and the kitchen were separated only slightly by half of a wall that made merely the suggestion of two separate spaces.

I left the room in a dramatic flurry, motioning her to join me as I retreated to the basement. It had been half finished to provide My Brother with a room. He was living in Stratford so he rarely used it except when he was home. I flung myself in front of the computer, which was really the only available chair in the room. She followed me and she sat on a laundry basket next to me.

"I'm so sorry," I said. "I can't believe he would say such stupid things."

Connected to the main room in the basement was a laundry room and a furnace room, and on the other side of the stairs was My Brother's room. The rage inside of me had snapped something. For some reason, this *felt like the last straw. I wanted something to change. I felt so powerless and confused. This needed to come out somehow. It felt like I was going to die if I continued to sit there and stew in silence. I stood up and walked into the furnace room with a kind of desperation that I had never known before. I don't know exactly why this was the breaking point for me but I felt at my limit of tolerance for his Jekyll and Hyde behaviour. He kept a bunch of tools in the furnace room. It was only a tiny amount of tools that he owned but I knew that if I looked for only a few seconds I would be able to find what I was looking for. I wanted something hard and small enough to cup in my hand. I wanted to do some damage.*

"What are you doing, dude?" my friend asked as I rummaged through the rusted silver tool box. I didn't answer her but continued to pick up and drop unsuitable objects until I wrapped my fist around a shiny steel tape measure that would do just the trick. I cupped it in my hand and smashed it repeatedly into my upper thigh. The pain

blossomed into my body like a dark creeping ivy and I felt a blissful relief from the pressure inside my heart and mind. It was almost like getting high. I was totally engrossed in the sensations until she grabbed my arms.

"Stop it!" she said. I didn't try to fight her and she looked directly into my eyes. "No," she repeated several times, shaking her head. For a moment I felt a flash of rage directed at her. She had a tree cut into her ankle almost the size of my hand and I had never tried to stop her from doing this. She took the tape measure from me and I ran out of gas.

I walked back into the main room and sat in front of the computer again. My friend resumed her seat on the laundry basket. I stared off into space feeling a terrible frozen emptiness creeping into my heart. It was that moment I decided something in my world had to change. I didn't know what or how, but going back to the way things were just seemed ludicrous.

"I can't stay here." she said.

"I don't blame you."

"I can't go home, either. I'm out past curfew and my mom would kill me."

"So what are you going to do?"

"I'm going to go sleep in the forest," she said. I liked that idea. I liked the drama of being homeless for a night. It seemed to make sense to me to make a strong enough statement about how miserable I felt. I was disturbed by the hardness spreading in my chest. I felt such little love for my father at that moment. It scared me. I knew that deep down I still loved him, but I couldn't actually feel it. I just felt a cold numbness.

I heard footsteps on the stairs and fear clutched my heart as I braced myself to be screamed at again. I could tell by the wait and gait of the foot falls it was my dad. He wasn't making angry noises. He rounded the winding staircase with a bowl in his hand, his movements were humble and apologetic. His gaze was cast down at the bowl in his hand as if he *was making sure he didn't drop his precious cargo. My friend looked at me for moral support and I watched him as he made his way down the last of the grey wooden steps and ambled towards us. His feet shuffled like an old man's, and you would never have gotten the sense of the powerful athlete he was by the way he moved in that moment.*

He set a bowl of strawberries down on the computer table between the two of us. The closeness of his body seemed to cut me at that moment and I just wanted him to be away from me. He mumbled some kind of apology and grovelled like a beaten dog. But I couldn't receive any of it. My anger had built up a tight wall and I was not able to accept anything from him at that moment. The whole situation seemed to increase my anger. The strawberries were considered a precious expensive food that I never would have taken for me and my friends. It was his olive branch. I felt insulted and unable to make any kind of kinship with him.

This kind of behaviour was normal for him; and it was normal for me to accept his apology, diffuse my rage, and continue on as if all was well. But this time I just couldn't. I was stuck in a mire of rage that had numbed my heart. After a few moments of trying, he retreated to the upstairs. I had won the siege for now.

"I'm going to sleep in the woods tonight," My friend said after a few moments of silence.

"I'm coming with you." I grabbed a thin pink knitted blanket from My Brother's room and left without telling my father. We didn't eat the strawberries.

Waking up with the dew set on our blanket was surprisingly cold for the time of year. My friend and I had cuddled up to each other for warmth and comfort. The pink blanket was somewhat threadbare and didn't do much to provide protection. It was just dawn and the sun was creeping through the trees. Beams of sunlight spun through the partitions of leaves and branches and danced with each gentle gust of wind. It was the beginning of a perfect July day in Southern Ontario. I could tell by my friend's breathing that she was also awake.

"Hey, dude," she whispered to me. "Do you want to go to my parent's house and finish sleeping?" The ground was hard and the setting dampness made it hard to sleep.

"Sure," I said.

We made our way to her house and slept there until noon. I had a job interview that day and I was supposed to meet my mother at the restaurant where she worked at around 4pm.

***

The day unfolded before me in a daze. My leg hurt as I limped around town to my interview and the emptiness in my heart kept me from enjoying the beautiful weather. The pain in my chest was so unbearable that I seemed to be protected from it as my body converted it to numbness.

My mother worked at a Chinese food restaurant. It was known for its excellent fare. My great-grandmother was visiting from out west and our friends, The Farmer and His Wife, were bringing her down to the restaurant to have dinner with me and my mother. Logically, I could return home to the farm with them, but I had decided to stay with my mother because I felt like hurting myself. I knew if I told her I needed supervision she would take me seriously. I had problems with suicidal thoughts and depression ever since the age of nine. It had been worse lately. I was frightened by the lack of feeling in my chest. I wanted to hurt myself just to feel something. I knew that if I continued on to pursue this morbid fascination with pain, it could turn into something really ugly. I wanted help.

I made it to the restaurant early. The Farmer and His Wife had yet to arrive with my great-grandmother. As my mom washed dishes between serving customers, I took the opportunity to talk with her about my issues with my dad.

I sat behind the counter chopping broccoli while mom ran between the kitchen and the dining room serving people. The restaurant was owned by a first generation Chinese immigrant with whom we had been friends for the last ten years. She was a tiny woman with the presence of a gentle battle commander. Her children called her The Q behind her back—a Star Trek reference suggesting the way she controlled the universe around her. They had even given her a mug with "The Q" on it, but she didn't get the joke. But overall, she was a loving matron, except during the dinner rush. At this moment, she was elbow deep in the wok, frying up her various standards to the hiss of the deep fryer. I had little appetite at this moment. It was a bad sign if I lost my appetite; it meant things were really bad.

The Farmer and His Wife arrived with my great-grandmother on time.

I had first met The Farmer and His Wife when I was taking Taekwon Do at a different martial arts studio. The Farmer had a charisma about him that drew a certain kind to him like iron filings to a magnet. It seemed that people either worshiped him or hated him and there were no in-betweens. He wasn't handsome. He had a weak jawline and a round button nose. But an incredible energy that oozed off of him created a glow of raw sexuality. He had a way of inserting a dirty joke or innuendo into conversation that created an air of sexual tension in the group. but at the same time seemed mostly harmless. He was sensitive enough, just enough, to push the boundaries without actually offending anyone.

His Wife was only 26 and they had been together since she was 18. She was a small pixi-ish woman with brown hair and blue eyes. Her features were kittenish and she had the idealized teenage figure with tiny breasts, small rounded hips and graceful limbs that ended in delicate hands and feet. Her weight was a scrutinized subject amongst the women who knew her. It was known that she weighed between 102-105 pounds on any given day. Though we criticized her for being skinny, a vicious vein of jealousy hung over the women as we gossiped about what she ate. She was sweet natured and always kind to me. She seemed to want to help whenever she could. She was rich and privileged and her family owned a plastics plant. She seemed to have this idea that she grew up poor, which was contradicted by the stories about years of gymnastics training and horseback riding and piano lessons. The Farmer's family were successful farmers.

Nothing seemed to penetrate the coldness that surrounded my heart. I couldn't lose myself in the pleasant country small talk that my mother and great-grandmother made with The Farmer and His Wife. I nodded and smiled at the right intervals. I could sense that everyone at the table, except for my great-grandmother, knew there was something wrong with me. I wanted them to know. I needed someone to notice that there was something wrong with me, and someone did.

The Farmer looked at me across the table; his eyes were penetrating shards of blue glass. I looked back at him. A silent communication transpired between us. I wanted him to be the one to rescue me.

When I was fifteen, I was training to compete in the National Taekwon-Do Championships. That year, The Farmer had befriended my mother and I and had taken on a small group of students out of our club to coach for the championships. The Headmaster of the club was too busy with more promising students, so he did not seem to mind the interest that The Farmer had taken in us, even though The Farmer was not an instructor at his club. He seemed to know what he was doing, though his style was much looser than the rigid form of Taekwon-Do ring fighting. The Farmer claimed to hold a black belt in Teakwon-Do and the equivalent to a black belt in a Filipino combat martial art called "Arnis." He could hold his own amongst the best of the fighters around our club.

After the championship, from which I took home a silver medal, The Headmaster and The Farmer had a falling out, which was never fully explained to me. The Headmaster came to me one day and told me never to speak to The Farmer again and that he was a bad man. I was devastated. I felt close to The Farmer. He supported me through the divorce of my parents. I was devoted to my master; but almost one year later, I would have a falling out with him, as well.

The Farmer seemed almost humoured by my suffering. He raised his hand to cover the side of his mouth in a strange attempt to share a secret with me.

"Are you feeling mellow?*" he said. I felt anything but mellow. Maybe dead inside, but not mellow. I nodded in agreement anyway. He smiled at me. He mouthed the words, "Are you stoned?"*

I shook my head. "I'm not feeling so good," I said.

"Oh."

Dinner was a blur to me. I ate my food without tasting it. I cradled the emptiness inside my chest like a baby. I couldn't lose myself in the simple pleasure of food and company. I wanted to keep this pain at the forefront of my mind right now just so I would be forced to make some kind of change. I didn't want to forget and go back to normal. I had no idea what to do.

We finished our meal and The Farmer and His Wife got ready to go.

"Are you getting a ride back with Them?" she asked. I would be alone except for my great-grandmother who would fall asleep on the couch leaving me alone with my thoughts.

"No, I'm going to stay here and wait for you to finish work. I need supervision." This last statement seemed to catch The Farmer's attention. He perked up.

"We can provide that," he said. He put his arm around His Wife. It was an answer to my prayers. They were so cool and interesting. I was just dying to spend more time with them. I was so touched that they would be interested in helping me with my problems. I loved The Farmer's attention. He made me feel important. I had a crush on him and I would bask in his attention when he listened to my problems. I thought that he would have some words of wisdom for me.

They seemed to have it all: money, friends, family and the respect of their community. I wanted their lives. They seemed so together and happy. His Wife was thin, attractive and married to a great man. They seemed so in love. I wanted to jump in their skin and just be them. At least I wanted to be His Wife. I wanted to be loved the way she was loved. If only I was as beautiful as she, someone would love me like that. But I would never be as beautiful as she was. She was skinny and perfect and cool. I was all lumps and cellulite and awkward teenage angst. I thought if I spent some time with them I could learn how to be as cool as they were. A ray of excitement began to thaw the carefully forged ice cage in which I had placed myself.

"Okay," I said, trying not to give away my excitement. "That would be nice." I could feel my sadness melting a bit. I wanted their attention. I still wanted them to sooth me, to comfort me.

They lived off the main road in a modest house with a large shop to the right. There was a nice size with a fenced in yard around the back. It was my first time over to their house and I was already impressed. I had never lived anywhere nice, so my standards were low. Simply owning a home of one's own was enough to amaze me. My father did own his own house but it was hard for me to relate that to wealth because of its state of perpetual squalor. I could tell right away that this home was well kept.

The garage door yawned open like a toothless metal mouth and there was a side door to the left that opened to the back yard. They entered through this way rather than the gate to prevent the dogs from escaping into the street. The shop had a grey concrete floor that looked like it was painful to fall on and the walls of the shop were lined with a variety of target pads and wooden swords that were used for martial arts training. My mother had been coming here to train for a while and I was now curious about what kind of drills and techniques they learned. I imagined it was intense.

"This is the shop," said The Farmer, and he gestured to the room. "It's where we train."

"Oh," I looked around, admiring the equipment.

His Wife went into the house carrying a package of some sort and he waved at me to follow her.

"Welcome to the palace," he said. I followed him into the back yard and found my way along a short stretch of patio that led to their back door. The back door opened to a landing and one had the option of going forward down a flight of stairs to the basement, veering to the left which led to a bathroom, or veering to the right which led to the kitchen and the rest of the house.

"Here, I'll give you the grand tour," he said, leaping past me into the kitchen as I removed my shoes. His Wife was bent over putting something away, her tiny round behind poking into the air. The Farmer reached out and slapped it hard. She yelped and gave him a look of exasperation. I couldn't tell if she was actually upset or just putting it on for my sake.

"Hey! Watch it!" she said.

"You wouldn't have said that if you were bent over naked," he said.

"If I was bent over naked I might have been expecting it," she said, and with a sigh, went back to adjusting the things in the cupboard. I thought she was being a poor sport about his playfulness. It thrilled me that he would be so sexual in front of me. It made me feel so mature. He chuckled as he gestured for me to follow him to the main floor. The living room was modestly decorated with tight industrial carpet and neutral walls but it still seemed fancy to me.

"So this is it," he said, dismissing the large room with a wave of his hand. "Let's go sit in the basement and cool off."

The stairs down to the basement were narrow and steep and it was noticeably cooler on the lower floor. To the right, there was a giant screen TV and couches curling around the walls. The Farmer flicked on the light and flopped onto the couch, sprawling his spider-thin form over them. Like the main floor, everything in the den was neutral but neat looking—except for the carpet, which was a mottled blue.

"So what's going on? You seemed mellow at the restaurant. I thought you might be smoking some grass," he said. I smiled at old-fashioned language. Nobody said "grass" anymore.

"No, I wasn't high. My dad and I had a fight last night and I ended up sleeping in the woods. I just couldn't be in the same house as him anymore."

"Oh, yeah. That sounds like trouble. It's a lot colder than you think, eh?"

"It is! My friend and I had to cuddle together for warmth." I said. I was so excited that he understood me.

"Yeah, I've spent a few nights on the street so I know that when it gets cold enough you stop caring about who you cuddle up with, even if it's

another guy," he said. I was in awe at his coolness. He had slept on the street and lived to tell the tale.

"So... Do you have a boyfriend?"

"No," I said blushing. I wished he was my boyfriend.

"Why not? Are you a lesbian?"

"I am bisexual." I said. I thought that would impress him. Maybe then he would regret marrying His Wife and wish he had married me.

"What?! Oh, that's just an excuse. I think you're a lesbian. Don't tell me you're a virgin, too. You're probably just a cock tease. You don't seem like the kind with the guts to put out."

"I am a virgin, but it's not by choice. I've tried to get laid but no guys want me."

"What are they, gay? *No, I think you're just a tease."*

"I am not!" This was so fun. But I didn't want him to think I was a tease. What a terrible thing to be. I wanted to be the kind of woman he admired. It felt so good to have his attention. My virginity seemed like a diseased appendage that I was trying to lop off. I was the last of my friends to lose it. They always teased me. I felt like such a loser.

He laughed at me. I felt like a silly child and he was humouring me. A man as cool and sexy as him would never want me. I hoped he thought I was hot, but that seemed absurd. How could a man with a smoking hot wife like the one he had upstairs, with her money and her perfect body, think I *was attractive in any way? I was really just a joke.*

"Well darlin', you have a few options here. You can stay here and talk to My Wife or you can come with me and get the tractor. What do you want?" he said, standing up and making his way to the stairs.

I thought for a few seconds. I liked His Wife but she was so boring compared to him. Basking in his attention was like the first rays of warm sunshine after a long night. It melted the frost around my heart and made me feel alive.

"I'll come with you," I said.

"Okay." And he bolted up the stairs two at a time.

Manufactured by Amazon.ca
Bolton, ON

45952316R00046